Over the Rainbow

The Story of Judy Garland

Ann Jungman

Illustrated by Lynn Willey

Judy, age 17

© 2004 **Pacific Learning**
© 2003 Written by **Ann Jungman**
Illustrated by **Lynn Willey c/o J. Martin and Artists**
Cover photo by **Sunset Boulevard/Sygma/Corbis UK Ltd.**
Photography: p. 1 Underwood & Underwood/Corbis UK Ltd.; p. 4
Bettmann/Corbis UK Ltd.; pp. 4–5 Corel; p. 5 Bettmann/Corbis
UK Ltd.; p. 6 Rex Features; p. 23 CinemaPhoto/Corbis UK Ltd.;
p. 26 Corbis UK Ltd.; p. 36 (top) Bettmann/Corbis UK Ltd.; p. 36
(bottom) Sunset Boulevard/Sygma/Corbis UK Ltd.; p. 37
Bettmann/Corbis UK Ltd.; p. 42 Bettmann/Corbis UK Ltd.; p. 44
Bettmann/Corbis UK Ltd.; p. 45 Hulton/Archive/Getty Images;
p. 46 Bettmann/Corbis UK Ltd.; pp. 46–47 Corel; p. 47
Bettmann/Corbis UK Ltd.
U.S. edit by **Rebecca McEwen**

This Americanized Edition of *Over the Rainbow,* originally
published in England in 2003, is published by arrangement
with Oxford University Press.

08 07 06 05 04
10 9 8 7 6 5 4 3 2 1

Published by
Pacific Learning
P.O. Box 2723
Huntington Beach, CA 92647-0723
www.pacificlearning.com

ISBN: 1-59055-396-9
PL-7415

Printed in China

Contents

Story Introduction

A star is born

The picture on the front of this book is the image of Judy Garland that most people recognize. It is from **The Wizard of Oz**, the film that made her a star.

However, what most people *don't* know is that the real-life Judy, who was born Frances Gumm, had a difficult, sometimes lonely life.

Judy's troubles began long before she was famous, and tormented her for the rest of her life. She was very close to her father, who died when Judy/Frances was still very young. Her relationship with her mother was not a very good one, and, as this book will show, it shaped Judy's entire life and career.

1938: Judy with her mother

Baby

Baby Frances Gumm

Judy Garland, who was born in 1922, was just two years old when she first stumbled on to the stage of her father's theater in Minnesota. Showing no fear, the toddler sang "Jingle Bells" for the crowd.

"Get the kid off the stage," someone yelled.

However, she sang the song three times before her father escorted her from the stage to cheers. So began one of the most amazing careers in show business.

Judy's real name was Frances Gumm. She was known as "Baby" – the youngest of Ethel and Frank Gumm's three daughters. Ethel was determined that one of her children would become a big star.

Ethel was forever insisting that the family get Frances out to Hollywood — and as quickly as possible.

Frank didn't agree. He thought it was more important for Frances and her sisters to have a simple, happy childhood. As far as he was concerned, fame could come later.

Frances was still so young that she didn't understand what her parents were talking about. All that she cared about was whether her parents were proud of her.

As her two older sisters, Jinny and Susie, congratulated Frances on her singing, she would just bury her head in her father's lap.

Her sisters knew that Frances had amazing talent. They also understood that their mother finally had the star material she'd been looking for. Now there was no stopping her ambition.

The family was going to leave their home and move to California.

Six weeks later, the family set off in their old Ford. They needed to earn money while they traveled, so every night, the family performed in whichever small town they found themselves.

It was 1925, before television, in the very early days of radio and movies. Good entertainment was difficult to find. Crowds would pack into the churches or community halls to see whatever was available.

First Frank would sing. He had a good voice and played the guitar beautifully. The crowd enjoyed that. Then the older girls, Jinny and Susie, would do a song and dance act, while Ethel played the piano. That went down well too. The crowd appreciated the youngsters.

After that, Ethel would sing. Unfortunately, the crowd hated her. They would boo and throw things on the stage. Frank and the family cringed with embarrassment.

The last act was Frances and her sisters. Then "Baby" had a small solo. The effect was always the same. The crowd cheered and called for more.

Ethel was convinced that Frances was going to be a smash in Hollywood. Her own problems faded away when she thought of her daughter's golden future.

On the Road

When the Gumm family finally arrived in Hollywood, things were not quite as golden as Ethel had dreamed. In fact, Hollywood turned out to be a difficult place to work and to live.

The family could only afford to rent one room. To make matters worse, the town was already full of mothers who believed their children were wonderfully talented.

Frank would point out these mothers to Ethel and beg her to reconsider. The mothers were unhappy, the children miserable. Frank just wanted to move his family back home.

Ethel agreed that he could leave if he wanted, but she was certain that Frances was special. She knew that if someone noticed Frances, their problems would be over.

So Ethel dressed little Frances in an ugly frilly dress and they joined the long lines waiting to be discovered.

Then every night, Ethel dragged exhausted Frances back to the one room they shared.

Before long, Frank was running out of money. He insisted that Ethel listen to reason. His daughters needed a proper home.

The three girls agreed. They hated living in Hollywood.

Ethel tried to argue. She insisted that Frances wanted to stay.

Poor little Frances just wanted to be with her father.

In the end, Frank used the last of his money to buy a small movie house in a desert town that was still within driving distance of Hollywood.

Before they left, Ethel signed up all the girls with the Melin Kiddies Agency. This agency was supposed to find work for child performers – and it did, in a way. All the girls were offered badly paid work at tiny theaters. However, by law, the two older ones had to go to school and could only perform on weekends.

The older girls' schedule was why Ethel pinned all her hopes on Frances. She dragged her from theater to theater, always hoping that some **talent scout** would happen to be at that particular performance.

Frances hated being away from her warm and loving father. Still, when she got on stage and started singing, somehow everything seemed all right. Audiences loved the plump little girl singing her heart out. And Frances loved them for loving her.

Frances was very lonely a lot of the time. The other child performers were usually quite a bit older. She had no one to play with or talk to.

Sometimes, desperate for a normal life, she would beg her mother to let her go home.

Her mother, who would get terribly angry at this, would ask whether or not she wanted to be a star.

Frances would just shake her head.

Ethel didn't care. She insisted that they keep traveling from theater to theater.

Frances would perform, and then she and Ethel would go back to some small, cheap hotel. Many nights, Frances cried uncontrollably.

Ethel would snap at her, and Frances would beg to see her sisters and father, whom she missed terribly.

Instead of comforting her daughter, Ethel would become enraged. She thought that Frances didn't care about how hard her mother worked. She often said that she would leave Frances at the hotel, all alone, if she didn't stop crying.

Poor Frances, worried that her mother might leave, would stop crying. She'd promise to be good and do whatever her mother wanted.

Ethel, still angry, didn't listen. She would walk out of the room and slam the door, leaving Frances on her own. Hours later, Ethel would return to find Frances shaking with fear.

Ethel demanded that Frances stop asking for her father. Frances would cry and cry as she promised to do whatever her mother asked of her.

Only then Ethel would put her daughter on her knee and comfort her. She knew that she had won.

CHAPTER

3

Judy Garland

Finally, there came a day that Frank had good news for Frances. He had bought a house just outside of Hollywood. Frances and her mother could finally leave behind their stormy days of staying in cheap motels. Frances could come home.

Frances couldn't believe it. She was finally going to live in a house, with her family – it was a dream come true for her.

Frances burst into tears. Only this time, they were tears of joy.

For the first time in her young life, Frances had plans she looked forward to.

First off, she asked if she could go to school. Her father quickly agreed, knowing how badly she wanted to go.

Ethel, however, had not given up on her ideas of stardom for her daughters. She sent all three of her girls to Mrs. Lawlor's School for Professional Students.

This was a school in Hollywood that was created specifically to teach children who wanted to be actors.

Each day, Frank would ask Frances how she was doing, and whether or not she liked her school. He wanted to know all about her life, and if she was making new friends.

There was one boy whom Frances liked, right from the start – a boy named Mickey Rooney.

Frances couldn't stop talking about him.

Mickey Rooney and Judy in 1940

He could sing and dance and was the funniest person she had ever met.

Little did Frances know that she would go on to star in many movies with Mickey Rooney. They would become best friends, and he stood by her through thick and thin.

Mickey was important, because Frances certainly needed friends.

Her parents' marriage went from bad to worse. Ethel shouted at Frank all the time. Frances cried as she listened to their fights, but Frank would hug his youngest daughter and try to comfort her.

One day, in an effort to try to make Frances happy, Frank bought her a dog, which is something she'd always dreamed of.

Frances adored him. If only her parents could get along, life would be almost normal.

Then one day Ethel announced to her family that the **World's Fair** was going to be held in Chicago. She believed that everyone in the world of show business was going to be there, and that the Gumm family needed to be there too.

Frank was upset. His daughters were finally getting settled in, and he couldn't believe that Ethel actually wanted to drag them off again.

Frances begged to stay with her father. As always, her mother ignored her requests.

As far as Ethel was concerned, a star needed to go where the work was. So she and her daughters headed for Chicago.

When they arrived in Chicago, Ethel decided to call the girls The Gumm Sisters.

Immediately, people told her that "The Gumm Sisters" name simply wouldn't work. After all, they would point out, "Gumm" rhymes with "dumb" and "crumb." It just wasn't a good name for the three lovely girls.

Finally, a famous comedian of the time named George Jessel had a suggestion.

Chicago World's Fair, 1933

He pointed to a pianist who was sitting close by, whose name was Robert Garland. Why not call them The Garland Sisters?

Ethel asked her daughers what they thought. The two older girls thought it sounded okay.

Frances hadn't been paying attention to the conversation, because she was enjoying the piano music. Her mother, who did not like being ignored, loudly asked her again what she thought.

Frances agreed that she wouldn't mind the name "The Garland Sisters." However, she had a request of her own. She asked if she could be called Judy, after the song she had been enjoying.

So little Frances Gumm became the legendary Judy Garland. Audiences loved her.

As Ethel watched her daughter perform in Chicago, she knew they were finally ready to storm Hollywood.

CHAPTER 4

Hollywood

When they got back home, Ethel took Judy around to all the movie studios.

She told everyone she met that her daughter sang like an angel.

Instead of agreeing with her, the agents and other show business professionals would tell her that Judy was too short, too plump, and too ordinary looking.

Ethel didn't care. She would drag Judy around tirelessly, and then beg people to simply listen to her sing. However, in Hollywood, singing wasn't enough. To be a star, a girl needed to *look* like an angel too.

Judy was terribly embarrassed as studio after studio rejected her.

Finally, when Judy was a young teenager, her luck changed. Roger Edens, a musician from the biggest of all the studios, Metro-Goldwyn-Mayer, telephoned. He wanted Judy to come in for an audition.

Judy was at home with her father. She was dressed in casual clothes, and was out playing with her dog.

Frank called out of the window that Metro wanted her for an audition, right away.

Judy knew her mother would be very angry if she messed this up. She struggled to get ready in the car as she and her father raced to the audition.

When Judy got to the studio, she sang "Zing Went the Strings of My Heart." Everyone in the room listened to her in stunned silence.

No one could believe that such a young girl could sing with such a tremendous voice, so packed with feeling.

Before long, the great Louis B. Mayer, the most powerful man in Hollywood, was called in to hear little Judy sing. When she finished, he clapped.

"She's no beauty," he famously said. "But she looks nice. She looks like the girl next door. I can use her."

Eventually, when she was fourteen, Judy signed with Metro-Goldwyn-Mayer. Ethel's dream was coming true – or it seemed to be.

Although it's true that Judy was signed on by a studio, she wasn't actually making movies. Instead, she was sent out to sing at the grand parties the famous stars gave.

One evening, Judy was booked to sing on the radio. Her beloved father, Frank, had a bad earache.

Judy didn't want to go sing. She wanted to stay with her father. Ethel was outraged. There was no way she was going to let her daughter miss this opportunity.

Frank tried to make Judy feel better. He told her to go, and that he would listen to her on the radio. He said he would be fine.

That evening, Judy sang her heart out for her father, but that night, Frank died.

For months, Judy cried herself to sleep every night. Now, there was no one to defend her against her mother's huge ambitions.

Every day, Judy went to the studio school. She liked school and loved being with her old friend, Mickey Rooney.

There was, however, a problem that Judy kept running up against at school.

Two of Judy's classmates were the stunningly beautiful Elizabeth Taylor and the equally lovely and talented Lana Turner. Compared to them, Judy felt ugly and

Elizabeth Taylor

grew more and more unhappy. In fact, Judy was a pretty girl. Unfortunately, she kept comparing herself to the great screen goddesses. Judy felt terrible about herself. Without her father's love and support, she grew more and more unhappy.

Lana Turner

Finally, Judy won a role starring in a film with Mickey Rooney. Mickey played an all-American boy named **Andy Hardy**. Judy played his next-door neighbor. In the film, Andy Hardy likes Judy, but he falls in love with other girls.

1938: "Love Finds Andy Hardy"

When Judy complained that this was like the story of her life, Andy tried to cheer her up. He told her that she was going to get a great role soon, and would be a bigger star than anybody from their school.

He was right. Judy's big break was just around the corner.

CHAPTER 5

Wizard of Oz

One morning, Judy's old friend Roger Edens asked to see her.

He was really excited. He told her that Metro had just purchased the rights to *The Wizard of Oz*. The studio thought it would make the greatest musical ever, and Roger thought that Judy would be perfect for the role of Dorothy.

Now Judy was excited too. She knew she would love to play that part.

Unfortunately, not everyone thought it was a great idea.

Louis B. Mayer told Judy that she was too old. Dorothy is ten years old in the book, and Judy was sixteen at the time. He also thought she was too plump.

Judy was devastated. Roger Edens told her to be patient. He knew the studio wouldn't find anyone else with a voice like hers.

Weeks later, Louis B. Mayer gave Judy the part, but he told her she needed to lose weight. For weeks, Judy ate nothing but chicken soup. Then the studio put her in tight corsets, but she still didn't look like a ten-year-old.

At this point, Mr. Mayer insisted that Judy start taking diet pills.

So Judy was put on diet pills. The weight fell off her – but now she could not sleep.

The studio then told her to start taking sleeping pills.

So Judy was given sleeping pills – but she had to be in the studio at five in the morning, and she was having a hard time waking up.

The studio then told her to take pills to "pep her up."

So, very much against her will, Judy began taking all sorts of different pills. They were to haunt her for the rest of her life.

Still, despite the corsets and the medication, Judy was happy. She loved playing Dorothy, the girl who finds herself on the yellow brick road, looking for the Wizard of Oz to help her get home to Kansas. No money was spared to make it the most spectacular film of its time. The sets were amazing. There were thousands of extras. Best of all, it had some great songs.

41

Now everyone was interested in Judy. Every day, journalists and photographers came to the studio to interview her. Her costars, playing the Cowardly Lion, the Tin Man, and the Scarecrow, were jealous of the attention she was getting. They made life as difficult for her as they could.

Margaret Hamilton and Judy Garland in "The Wizard of Oz," 1939

The only person who helped Judy was the actress who played the Wicked Witch of the West, Margaret Hamilton.

When the studio bosses saw the film, they were delighted with everything but one of the songs.

As strange as it may seem, they wanted to cut out "Somewhere Over the Rainbow." Some thought it didn't have a good tune. Others just thought that people wouldn't like the words.

Cast members pose by a giant promotional poster for "The Wizard of Oz"

Judy and Roger Edens had to fight hard for their favorite song. At last, it was left in, but only after the bosses were sure that everyone liked it.

They did like it. In fact, people liked the whole movie. It was the most successful movie Hollywood had ever seen, and Judy as Dorothy was a megastar.

From rising star...

The movie is now a classic. Maybe Dorothy's search for happiness rang a bell for Judy Garland. She put her whole soul into a part for which she will always be remembered.

As for "Somewhere Over the Rainbow," it became a classic too. It is one of the most popular songs ever, and it will always remind people of a timeless Judy Garland.

... to the best there is!

Story Background

Young Judy on a pony

Judy Garland has been described as looking very much like "the girl next door." This means that, compared to many of her fellow performers, Judy was considered pretty, but not beautiful. What do you think?

As a little girl, Judy's mother pushed her into a very competitive world. She was regularly told that she was too plump. This, and the fact that at sixteen years old she was playing the part of a ten-year-old in *The Wizard of Oz,* pushed Judy into unhealthy habits for life.

Thirteen-year-old Judy having some fun!

Judy's need to take pills to stay slim, to help her sleep, and then to wake up again were common practices at the time. Many actresses struggled with this, but perhaps none more so than Judy.

Despite her troubles, though, Judy Garland was a talented and extraordinary person.

Index

Glossary

Andy Hardy – Judy Garland began her acting career in the film series of this name in 1935

talent scout – a person whose job it is to discover and recruit people with talent or particular skills

Wizard of Oz – Judy Garland became a movie star when she performed in this film in 1939

World's Fair – this international showpiece was held in Chicago in 1933, and was called "A Century of Progress." It was an enormous event!